A personal collection of poems

Dhanya Patel

India | USA | UK

Presentation by *BookLeaf Publishing*

Web: www.bookleafpub.com

E-mail: info@bookleafpub.com

ISBN: 9789357214698

First edition 2022

*I'd like to dedicate this book to all the poets
I have read the works of before. I will
forever appreciate your contribution.*

ACKNOWLEDGEMENT

Firstly, I want to acknowledge the many websites and online resources that helped me when I struggled to fit words into a syllable count, or needed to find words that rhyme well. I would also like to thank Pinterest, for all the aesthetic images that I used, and collected throughout this time. It really helped me in tackling writer's block and garnering inspiration for many of these poems. I feel slightly upset that I won't have an excuse to sit for hours scrolling on there anymore. However, this experience has opened my eyes to poetry and all the fantastic versions and rules that apply throughout history, as a result of this I enjoy poetry and overall literature a lot more.

Tanka (Classical Japanese form)

I watch through the glass,
as rain pours down the window,
joining, gathering,
it winds and curves and trickles,
slowly making its way back

Gogyohka (Off-shoot of Tanka form)

A street full of unique shops
But one stands out more than others,
An awkward corner plot.
Strange as it appears, the monotonous building
is covered from roof to ground
In a healthy plethora of vivacious flora

Otava Rima (of Italian origins)

Imagine a place only the books told,
where perennials grow between lush grass,
upon a hill sits an oak tree of old,
though the indecisive seasons may pass,
yorkshire fog shall always cling, stick and hold,
as the buttercups and clovers outlast,
rosy tulips within my memory.
I never want to leave this reverie.

Haiku (Originated in Japan)

Fairytales of old
printed in letters of gold
with secrets untold

Shadorma (alleged origins in Spain)

Abruptly
A paralian
Is shoved far
Too close for
Ones comfort to a wrathful
Tempest of distress

Spenserian stanza (French and Italian origins)

Stirring, churning, turning the spatula
how to make a cake is what I'm learning
so far I've not seen the tarantula
left unattended, this is concerning
I leave to check but am soon returning
too much of my time spent taking
care that I do not find the cake burning
since this is my very first time baking
I hope that I can do some good decorating

Villanelle (French origins)

A gentle warmth returns to the land in spring
Along with it a flurry of new baby chicks
Verdant leaves and delicate blossoms bloom in
Beijing
A symbol of renewal, billowy petals of various
white, yellow and pinks bring
Along a multitude of emotion, a sense that
predicts
The beginning of new life in spring
From the return of florescent flowers to beautiful
butterflies whose wing
Learns the careful way of the breeze, that does
not trick
Sulphur cosmos of deep, rich oranges line
streams in Beijing
Early April is the best time to witness full
blossoms sing
Within the Jinzhan tulip garden, where a painter
portrays a mix
Of kaleidoscopic hues of flora in spring
Among the array of magnolias from deep purple
to pure white, tree sparrows cling
To a branch high in the sky overlooking cleverly
constructed bricks

Tourists flock to botanical gardens all over
Beijing
To witness the majestic Hoopoe perching like a
king
A royal sight to see, rare as a total eclipse
Delight in the captivating show of spring
Which looks most wonderful in Beijing

Rispetto (Italian origins)

he'd make you believe this is hell
torturing with screeching white chalk
when will you finally ring bell?
with his boring ted talk
scowling at our fatigued faces
as he swiftly takes three paces
we wish that the time would pass quick
of this mundane class we are sick

Cinquain (Medieval French origins)

Tea pots
filled with dried leaves
made of heavy iron
storing moments from much too
long ago

Limerick (Unknown)

I once met a brilliant duck
Whose name to my shock was Ben Chuck
He had not a clue
That stuck to his shoe
Was a massive red fire truck

Acrostic (Greek origins)

Narcissistic
Alluring
Therapeutic
Unforgiving
Rich
Expansive

Sijo (Korean origins)

Autumn-shaded maple leaves, fall gracefully
into the stream
Between rocks and pebbles, dusted in verdant
moss which water
Trickles peacefully from, within valleys in the
distant background

Triolet (French origin)

Stunning was the view of the lake by twilight
The mellow radiance of the sky calming
Sitting among the soft glow from fireflies was
the highlight
Stunning was the view of the lake by twilight
Although this paradise-like state finite,
The ripples in water extremely charming
Stunning was the view of the lake by twilight
The mellow radiance of the sky claming

Decima (Origins in Spain and Latin America)

Minty red and white candy canes
Delicious festive gingerbread
and with that Christmas spirit spread
when you play long-winded board games,
from working race cars to toy trains
one thing is obviously clear
Now that Christmas is very near
Everybody is giving gifts
Listening to radio hits
The most wonderful time of year

Kimo (Israeli version of a haiku)

On this dark and misty night before me, I look out from my window to the lake,

I can not dive into the waters

For I do not want to disturb the breathtaking beauty of the moonglade upon the lake

Sensory (Unknown)

17

I can see in the distance a small white cottage
I can hear squawking seagulls flying high above
I can feel on the tips of my fingers the wisps of
wild grass
I can taste salt sprayed from the nearby sea
I can smell

Dodoitsu (Japanese origins)

I once heard of a cursed ring
Made of polished bright green jade
Smooth as a piece of silk cloth
But much more lethal

Cherita (Malay origins, created recently)

Mountains are made naturally.

For people to live up and beyond the clouds,
Far from the general population.

Why sit on a high horse when you can live on
top of a mountain?
Where things are simply much better.

Imayo (Japanese origins)

Lilac wisteria hang - obscuring the view
Sturdy branches that coil well - wrap around
pillars
A soft breeze passes calmly - making the
flowers
Flutter beautifully along - in the setting sun

Tricube (Western variant of Haiku)

Cloudy skies
Dictate moods
Stunningly

But I've heard
That if you
Take out time

To value
Smaller things
You'll be glad

Rime couee (French origins)

Cinnamon apple scented candles
Finally time to ditch sandals
Burnt orange shaded leaves
Dried to a crisp falling from trees
Still not yet cold enough to freeze
A warm blanket she weaves